AF809645

# 51 Must Know Facts About Albert Einstein

# BESTSELLING NON-FICTION

- Gravity by George Gamow
  Sciences/Physics, ISBN: 9789388118705
- How to Develop Self-Confi. and Pub. Speaking by Dale Carnegie
  Mind, Body & Spirit, ISBN: 9789388118286
- How to Stop Worrying and Start Living by Dale Carnegie
  Mind, Body & Spirit, ISBN: 9789387669161
- How to Win Friends and Influence People by Dale Carnegie
  Self Help/General, ISBN: 9789387669178
- Mein Kampf by Adolf Hitler
  Autobiographies/Leaders, ISBN: 9789387669260
- My Experiments with Truth by Mahatma Gandhi
  Autobiographies/Leaders, ISBN: 9789387669277
- Relativity by Albert Einstein
  Sciences/Physics, ISBN: 9789387669185
- The Art of War by Sun Tzu
  Self Help/Success, ISBN: 9789387669321
- The Diary of a Young Girl by Anne Frank
  Autobiographies/Memoirs, ISBN: 9789387669208
- The Magic of Believing by Claudie Bristol
  Religion/Christianity, ISBN: 9789388118217
- The Miracles of Your Mind by Joseph Murphy
  Mind, Body & Spirit, ISBN: 9789387669215
- The Power of Your Subconscious Mind by Joseph Murphy
  Mind, Body & Spirit, ISBN: 9789387669222
- The Richest Man in Babylon by George S. Clason
  Business & Economics, ISBN: 9789388118354
- Think and Grow Rich by Napoleon Hill
  Self Help/Success, ISBN: 9789387669352

**Search the book by its ISBN**

# 51 Must Know Facts About

# ALBERT EINSTEIN

GENERAL PRESS

*Published by*
**GENERAL PRESS**
4805/24, Fourth Floor, Krishna House
Ansari Road, Daryaganj, New Delhi - 110002
Ph : 011-23282971, 45795759
E-mail : generalpressindia@gmail.com

**www.generalpress.in**

© General Press

All rights reserved. No part of this publication may be reproduced, stored in a retrieval system, or transmitted, in any form or by any means—electronic, mechanical, photocopying, recording or otherwise—without the prior written permission of the publishers.

First Edition : 2022

ISBN : 9789354992285

Published by Azeem Ahmad Khan for General Press

# Contents

# *Introduction*

Albert Einstein was one of the best ingenious scientists and masterminds in human history. A century ago, his remarkable published theory of General Relativity created new ideas related to the evolution of the universe and black holes, altered our knowledge of gravity, time and space dramatically. The physicist's equation that helped explain special relativity $E = MC^2$ is eminent even among those who do not understand its underlying physics.

Einstein received the Nobel Prize for Physics in the year 1921. He received the coveted prize for his explanation of the photoelectric effect and not on his ideas of relativity as then they were considered questionable, though during his acceptance speech, Einstein still opted to speak about relativity. He also tried in vain to unify all the forces of the universe in a single theory, or a theory of everything, which he was still working on at the time of his death. His extraordinary brilliant mind was advanced with creativity and allowed him to see possibilities, not limitations. He was also fuelled by an unquenchable thirst to discover, explore and indulge his curiosity. His wisdom has never been more pertinent to entrepreneurs, creators and innovators.

After his death, while performing the autopsy, Princeton pathologist Thomas Harvey extracted the scientist's brain and kept it aside in the hope of unlocking the secrets of his genius. Later, after he was able to get approval of Einstein's son, Harvey chopped the brain into pieces and sent it to various scientists for research. In the year 1999, a team from a Canadian University published a paper declaring Einstein possessed unusual folds on his parietal lobe, a part of the brain that is associated with mathematical and spatial ability.

*51 Must Know Facts about Albert Einstein* will take you on a journey to the life of the most prolific influencer of the 20th Century. Comprehend on the Brainiac that Einstein was, his profound life, and his incredible discoveries that contributed effectively to the world we live in today.

# 51 MUST KNOW FACTS ABOUT ALBERT EINSTEIN

## FACT NUMBER

# 1

Einstein didn't start speaking until the age of 3 or 4. When he did, his first sentence was to complain at dinner that the soup was too hot. When asked why he hadn't spoken before then, he replied: "because up to now, everything was in order."

FACT NUMBER

# 2

Einstein was born on March 14, 1879, in Ulm, Württemberg, Germany. He grew up in a secular Jewish family. His father, Hermann Einstein, was a salesman and engineer who, with his brother, founded Elektrotechnische Fabrik J. Einstein & Cie, a Munich-based company that mass-produced electrical equipment. Einstein's mother, the former Pauline Koch, ran the family household. Einstein had one sister, Maja, born two years after him.

FACT NUMBER

# 3

Up until he was 9, Einstein would think through what he wanted to say before speaking. He preferred to practice his sentences in his head or under his breath until he got them right.

## FACT NUMBER

# 4

Einstein was born with what his family thought was an abnormally oversized head. The doctor was able to convince them that his body would catch up. Once it did, his grandmother complained to his parents he was too fat.

## FACT NUMBER

# 5

Einstein attended elementary school at the Luitpold Gymnasium in Munich. However, he felt alienated there and struggled with the institution's rigid pedagogical style. He also had what were considered speech challenges, though he developed a passion for classical music and playing the violin, which would stay with him into his later years. Most consequently, Einstein's youth was marked by deep inquisitiveness and inquiry.

## FACT NUMBER

# 6

Einstein was a talented violinist. He began music lessons at the age of 5, but fell in love with music when he discovered Mozart's violin sonatas at the age of 13. His violin was nicknamed "Lina", and he said that the most joy in his life came from his violin.

FACT NUMBER

# 7

Some researchers claimed that Einstein had a mild manifestation of autism or Asperger's syndrome.

## FACT NUMBER

# 8

At the age of 15, Einstein's refusal to bend to the authority of one of his teachers led to him being kicked out of class. In college, he irritated his professors with his impertinence, never hiding the fact that he found their classes boring.

## FACT NUMBER

# 9

Einstein would write in his memoirs that two "wonders" deeply affected his early years, according to Hans-Josef Küpper, an Albert Einstein scholar. Young Einstein encountered his first wonder—a compass—at the age of 5: He was mystified that invisible forces could deflect the needle. This would lead to a lifelong fascination with unseen forces. The second wonder came at the age of 12 when he discovered a book of geometry, which he worshipped, calling it his "holy geometry book."

## FACT NUMBER

# 10

Towards the end of the 1880s, Max Talmud, a Polish medical student who sometimes dined with the Einstein family, became an informal tutor to young Einstein. Talmud had introduced his pupil to a children's science text that inspired Einstein to dream about the nature of light. Thus, during his teens, Einstein penned what would be seen as his first major paper, "The Investigation of the State of Aether in Magnetic Fields."

## FACT NUMBER

# 11

Hermann Einstein relocated the family to Milan, Italy, in the mid-1890s after his business lost out on a major contract. Einstein was left at a relative's boarding house in Munich to complete his schooling at the Luitpold Gymnasium. Faced with military duty when he turned of age, Einstein allegedly withdrew from classes, using a doctor's note to excuse himself and claim nervous exhaustion. With their son rejoining them in Italy, his parents understood Einstein's perspective but were concerned about his future prospects as a school dropout and draft dodger.

## FACT NUMBER

# 12

Einstein was not actually a poor student. He never "failed math." At age 16, he failed his entrance exam to the Federal Polytechnic School in Zurich, but only because he struggled with the non-science subjects (especially French). Einstein continued to study and was able to attend the school the following year.

## FACT NUMBER

# 13

After graduating, Einstein faced major challenges in terms of finding academic positions, having alienated some professors over not attending class more regularly in lieu of studying independently. Einstein eventually found steady work in 1902 after receiving a referral for a clerk position in a Swiss patent office. While working at the patent office, Einstein had the time to further explore ideas that had taken hold during his studies at the Swiss Federal Institute of Technology and thus cemented his theorems on what would be known as the principle of relativity.

FACT NUMBER

# 14

In 1905—seen by many as a "miracle year" for the theorist—Einstein had four papers published in the *Annalen der Physik*, one of the best-known physics journals of the era. Two focused on the photoelectric effect and Brownian motion. The two others, which outlined $E=MC^2$ and the special theory of relativity, were defining Einstein's career and the course of the study of physics.

FACT NUMBER

# 15

Einstein was eventually able to gain admission into the Swiss Federal Institute of Technology in Zurich, specifically due to his superb mathematics and physics scores on the entrance exam. He was still required to complete his pre-university education first, and thus attended a high school in Aarau, Switzerland helmed by Jost Winteler. Einstein lived with the schoolmaster's family and fell in love with Winteler's daughter, Marie. Einstein later renounced his German citizenship and became a Swiss citizen at the dawn of the new century.

## FACT NUMBER

# 16

Einstein was the first to discover the equation that showed the universe is expanding, but he thought it was a mistake. Years later, Hubble's telescope confirmed that the theory of relativity was correct, and his biggest blunder was thinking he was wrong!

## FACT NUMBER

# 17

Einstein married Mileva Maric on January 6, 1903. While attending school in Zurich, Einstein met Maric, a Serbian physics student. Einstein continued to grow closer to Maric, but his parents were strongly against the relationship due to her ethnic background. Nonetheless, Einstein continued to see her, with the two developing a correspondence via letters in which he expressed many of his scientific ideas. Einstein's father passed away in 1902, and the couple married shortly thereafter. That same year the couple had a daughter, Lieserl, who might have been later raised by Maric's relatives or given up for adoption. Her ultimate fate and whereabouts remain a mystery. The couple had two sons, Hans Albert Einstein (who became a well-known hydraulic engineer) and Eduard "Tete" Einstein (who was diagnosed with schizophrenia as a young man).

## FACT NUMBER

# 18

The Einstein's marriage would not be a happy one, with the two divorcing in 1919 and Maric having an emotional breakdown in connection to the split. During his marriage to Maric, Einstein had also begun an affair some time earlier with a cousin, Elsa Löwenthal. The couple wed in 1919, the same year of Einstein's divorce. He would continue to see other women throughout his second marriage, which ended with Löwenthal's death in 1936.

## FACT NUMBER

# 19

Einstein played around with an alternative to the big bang theory. The theory proposed that the universe expanded steadily and eternally instead of all at once in a big bang. Einstein later abandoned the theory, and the paper was never published.

FACT NUMBER

# 20

Einstein paid his wife Mileva his entire prize money from his Nobel Prize, a staggering $32,250 which was vastly more than a professor's salary back then.

FACT NUMBER

# 21

In 1921, Einstein won the Nobel Prize for Physics for his explanation of the photoelectric effect, since his ideas on relativity were still considered questionable. He wasn't actually given the award until the following year due to a bureaucratic ruling, and during his acceptance speech, he still opted to speak about relativity.

## FACT NUMBER

# 22

As a physicist, Einstein had many discoveries, but he is perhaps best known for his theory of relativity and the equation $E=MC^2$, which foreshadowed the development of atomic power and the atomic bomb.

## FACT NUMBER

# 23

Fearing a German nuclear bomb, Einstein wrote a letter to President Roosevelt encouraging him to work on a nuclear weapon. This led to the creation of the Manhattan project, which was responsible for the atomic bomb. His famous equation $E = MC^2$ also made the bomb theoretically possible.

FACT NUMBER

# 24

Einstein first proposed a special theory of relativity in 1905 in his paper, "On the Electrodynamics of Moving Bodies," taking physics in an electrifying new direction. By November 1915, Einstein completed the general theory of relativity. Einstein considered this theory the culmination of his life research. He was convinced of the merits of general relativity because it allowed for a more accurate prediction of planetary orbits around the sun, which fell short in Isaac Newton's theory, and for a more expansive, nuanced explanation of how gravitational forces worked. Einstein's assertions were affirmed via observations and measurements by British astronomers Sir Frank Dyson and Sir Arthur Eddington during the 1919 solar eclipse, and thus a global science icon was born.

FACT NUMBER

# 25

Formulated by Albert Einstein in 1905, the theory of relativity is the notion that the laws of physics are the same everywhere. The theory explains the behavior of objects in space and time, and it can be used to predict everything from the existence of black holes, to light bending due to gravity, to the behavior of the planet Mercury in its orbit.

FACT NUMBER

# 26

His great breakthroughs came from experiments performed in his head rather than in the lab. Einstein performed thought experiments. At a young age, he tried to picture in his mind, what it would be like to ride alongside the light beam.

FACT NUMBER

# 27

Einstein's 1905 paper on the matter/energy relationship proposed the equation $E=MC^2$: the energy of a body (E) is equal to the mass (M) of that body times the speed of light squared (C2). This equation suggested that tiny particles of matter could be converted into huge amounts of energy, a discovery that heralded atomic power.

FACT NUMBER

# 28

Einstein believed in God. He defined God in an objective fashion but believed that God's work is reflected in the 'harmony of nature's laws and the beauty of all that exists.

## FACT NUMBER

# 29

Albert Einstein was known as the "people's scientist" because of his pragmatic sense of humour and his approachable manner. His hair was always uncombed, clothing scruffy, and he never wore socks—not even when visiting President Roosevelt at the White House.

## FACT NUMBER

# 30

In 1952, Albert Einstein was offered the chance to be President of Israel. He turned down the offer insisting that he was unqualified.

## FACT NUMBER

# 31

Einstein started a small discussion group called 'The Olympia Academy,' with some of his friends to discuss science and philosophy while he was unemployed. He came up with the theory of relativity at around this time.

FACT NUMBER

# 32

Einstein loved to smoke. He believed that pipe smoking "contributes to a somewhat calm and objective judgment in all human affairs." He gave up smoking on doctor's instructions, but didn't give up the pipes themselves. He would often stick one into his mouth and chew on it.

## FACT NUMBER

# 33

Einstein loved to sail. His boat was called "Tinef" which is Yiddish for worthless or junk, and it equally described his sailing skills. Not only was he a lousy sailor, but he didn't even know how to swim!

## FACT NUMBER

# 34

Einstein's brain was overall smaller than average, but the parietal lobes were 15% wider than normal. These areas are linked to mathematical ability, and visual and spatial awareness. Researchers believe that this is why Einstein tackled scientific thought the way he did.

FACT NUMBER

# 35

As he left his 72nd birthday party, Einstein was surrounded by photographers. Tired of fake smiling, he stuck his tongue out instead. Einstein ordered 9 pictures for personal use, and signed one of them for a reporter. That photograph sold at an auction for $74,324!

## FACT NUMBER

# 36

Einstein never had a car of his own, and he never learned to drive. If he needed to go somewhere by car, he had friends or a chauffeur drove him.

## FACT NUMBER

# 37

In December of 1932, the FBI started keeping a file on Einstein. At the time of his death, the file was 1427 pages long. Then FBI director J. Edgar Hoover was deeply suspicious of Einstein, and believed he was an extreme radical and a communist.

FACT NUMBER

# 38

Towards the end of WWII, Einstein had a passionate affair with Margarita Konenkova – a brilliant scientist and Russian spy. Their affair only ended when she and her husband returned to Moscow in 1945. Konenkova was allegedly tasked with learning about and "influencing" the American nuclear program, and was instructed to get close to J. Robert Oppenheimer of the Manhattan Project. Einstein was not directly involved in the Manhattan Project, so it's not entirely clear what Konenkova was hoping to get out of him.

## FACT NUMBER

# 39

Einsteinium is the 99th element on the periodic table. It's named after Albert Einstein, though he actually had nothing to do with its discovery or research.

FACT NUMBER

# 40

After moving to the United States, Einstein became an active member of the NAACP (National Association for the Advancement of Colored People), and courageously took a public stand against racial segregation in America.

FACT NUMBER

# 41

In 1923, Einstein travelled to Jerusalem to present the first scientific address at the Hebrew University he had helped to fund. At one of his speaking engagements, he declared: "I consider this the greatest day of my life".

## FACT NUMBER

# 42

Einstein's wife Elsa managed his fan mail and collected $1.00 for an autograph and $5.00 for a photograph. Einstein donated the proceeds to charity.

FACT NUMBER

# 43

Einstein tirelessly wrote letters to Presidents, prime ministers, and other leaders asking them to take in unemployed German-Jewish scientists during the Nazi regime. His letters saved over 1,000 Jews from persecution and the Nazi camps. He also wrote a now-famous letter to FDR shortly before figuring out uranium-powered nuclear chain reactions, which would power the atomic bombs.

## FACT NUMBER

# 44

After the US dropped the atomic bomb on Hiroshima and Nagasaki in 1945, Einstein became active in the political movement to prevent the use of atomic bombs in the future.

## FACT NUMBER

# 45

A Nazi magazine in Germany printed an enemies list, and Einstein was on it listed as "Not Yet Hanged." It also offered a $5000 Bounty for his head.

## FACT NUMBER

# 46

Einstein realized his life was at risk after Hitler assumed power in Germany. Einstein fled to Belgium, where he learned that his boat and cottage had been seized. He then escaped to England, and he was kept under armed protection until he found safety in America.

## FACT NUMBER

# 47

Einstein said: "If a cluttered desk is a sign of a cluttered mind, of what, then, is an empty desk a sign?" A famous photograph taken on the day he died showed bulging book shelves, a desk cluttered with notebooks, journals, a pipe & a tobacco tin.

FACT NUMBER

# 48

Right before he died, Einstein uttered his final words to a nurse. Unfortunately, the words were spoken in German—a language the nurse didn't speak or understand.

## FACT NUMBER

# 49

Einstein died of an aortic aneurysm on April 18, 1955. A blood vessel burst near his heart, according to the American Museum of Natural History (AMNH). When asked if he wanted to have surgery, Einstein refused. "I want to go when I want to go," he said. "It is tasteless to prolong life artificially. I have done my share; it is time to go. I will do it elegantly."

## FACT NUMBER

# 50

Einstein had a terrible memory for details he deemed unimportant. When questioned about why he had to look up his phone number, Einstein replied: "Why should I memorize something I can so easily get from a book?"

## FACT NUMBER

# 51

Einstein's body—most of it, anyway—was cremated; his ashes were spread in an undisclosed location, according to the AMNH. However, a doctor at Princeton Hospital, Thomas Harvey, had performed an autopsy, apparently without permission, and removed Einstein's brain and eyeballs, according to Matt Blitz, who wrote about Einstein's brain in a 2015 column for Today I Found Out.

# OTHER HARDBACK BOOKS

- 1984 by George Orwell
  Fiction/Classics, ISBN: 9788193545836
- Abraham Lincoln by Lord Charnwood
  Biographies/Leaders, ISBN: 9789387669147
- Alice's Adventures in Wonderland by Lewis Carroll
  Children's/Classics, ISBN: 9789387669055
- Animal Farm by George Orwell
  Fiction/Classics, ISBN: 9789387669062
- Anthem by Ayn Rand
  Fiction/Classics, ISBN: 9789389157178
- As a Man Thinketh by James Allen
  Fiction/Classics, ISBN: 9789388118422
- Awakened Imagination by Neville Goddard
  Religion & Spirituality, ISBN: 9789389157185
- Be What You Wish by Neville Goddard
  Mind, Body & Spirit, ISBN: 9789388118163
- Becoming a Writer by Dorothea Brande
  Self Help/General, ISBN: 9789389157192
- Believe in Yourself by Joseph Murphy
  Mind, Body & Spirit, ISBN: 9789388118439
- Black Beauty by Anna Sewell
  Children's/Classics, ISBN: 9789388118262
- Civilization and Its Discontents by Sigmund Freud
  Social Sciences/General, ISBN: 9789388118279
- Demian by Hermann Hesse
  Fiction/Classics, ISBN: 9789388118170
- Feeling is the Secret by Neville Goddard
  Religion & Spirituality, ISBN: 9789389157208

**Search the book by its ISBN**

# OTHER HARDBACK BOOKS

- Gitanjali by Rabindranath Tagore
  Fiction/Poems, ISBN: 9789387669079
- Great Speeches of Abraham Lincoln by Abraham Lincoln
  History/United States, ISBN: 9789387669154
- How to Attract Money by Joseph Murphy
  Self Help/Success, ISBN: 9789388118446
- How to be Filled with the Holy Spirit by A.W. Tozer
  Religion/Christianity, ISBN: 9789389157215
- How to Enjoy Your Life and Your Job by Dale Carnegie
  Self Help/General, ISBN: 9789388118293
- Illust. Biography of William Shakespeare by Manju Gupta
  Biographies/Authors, ISBN: 9789387669246
- Madhubala by Manju Gupta
  Biographies/Cinems, ISBN: 9789387669253
- Mansarover 1 (Hindi) by Premchand
  Fiction/Short Stories, ISBN: 9789387669086
- Meditations by Marcus Aurelius
  Non Fiction/Philosopy, ISBN: 9789388118781
- My Inventions: The Autobio. of Nikola Tesla by Nikola Tesla
  Autobiographies/Scientists, ISBN: 9789388118187
- Selected Stories of Rabindranath Tagore by Rabindranath Tagore
  Fiction/Short Stories, ISBN: 9789387669307
- Sense and Sensibility by Jane Austen
  Fiction/Classics, ISBN: 9789387669109
- Siddhartha by Hermann Hesse
  Fiction/Classics, ISBN: 9789387669116
- Tales from India by Rudyard Kipling
  Fiction/Short Stories, ISBN: 9789387669123

**Search the book by its ISBN**

# OTHER HARDBACK BOOKS

- The Alchemy of Happiness by Al-Ghazzali
  Religion & Spirituality, ISBN: 9789388118309

- Tales from Shakespeare by Charles Lamb, Mary Lamb
  Fiction/Short Stories, ISBN: 9789387669314
- The Alchemy of Happiness by Al-Ghazzali
  Religion & Spirituality, ISBN: 9789388118309
- The Art of Public Speaking by Dale Carnegie
  Self Help/General, ISBN: 9789388118477
- The Autobiography of a Yogi by Paramahansa Yogananda
  Autobiographies/General, ISBN: 9789387669192
- The Dynamic Laws of Prosperity by Catherine Ponder
  Mind, Body & Spirit, ISBN: 9789388118194
- The Elements of Style by William Strunk
  Non Fiction/Skill, ISBN: 9789389157222
- The Game of Life and How to Play It by Florence Scovel Shinn
  Mind, Body & Spirit, ISBN: 9789388118316
- The Imitation of Christ by Thomas À Kempis
  Religion/Christianity, ISBN: 9789388118200
- The Jungle Book by Rudyard Kipling
  Children's/Classics, ISBN: 9789387669338
- The Knowledge of the Holy by A.W. Tozer
  Religion/Christianity, ISBN: 9789389157239
- The Light of Asia by Sir Edwin Arnold
  Fiction/Poetry, ISBN: 9789387669130
- The Magic of Faith by Joseph Murphy
  Mind, Body & Spirit, ISBN: 9789388118712
- The Origin of Species by Charles Darwin
  Sciences/Life Sciences, ISBN: 9789387669345
- The Path of Prosperity by James Allen
  Mind, Body & Spirit, ISBN: 9789388118323

**Search the book by its ISBN**

# OTHER HARDBACK BOOKS

- The Power of Awareness by Neville Goddard
  Mind, Body & Spirit, ISBN: 9789388118330
- The Power of Concentration by Theron Q. Dumont
  Self Help/General, ISBN: 9789388118224
- The Power of Positive Thinking by Norman Vincent Peale
  Mind, Body & Spirit, ISBN: 9789388118729
- The Prophet by Kahlil Gibran
  Fiction/Classics, ISBN: 9789388118453
- The Psychopathology of Everyday Life by Sigmund Freud
  Non Fiction/Psychology, ISBN: 9789388118231
- The Pursuit of God by A.W. Tozer
  Religion/Christianity, ISBN: 9789389157246
- The Quick and Easy Way to Effec. Speaking by Dale Carnegie
  Self Help/General, ISBN: 9789388118347
- The Science of Getting Rich by Wallace D. Wattles
  Self Help/Success, ISBN: 9789387669239
- The Seven Laws of Teaching by John Milton Gregory
  Self Help/General, ISBN: 9789388118460
- The Upanishads by Swami Paramananda
  Religion/Hinduism, ISBN: 9789388118774
- The World as I See It by Albert Einstein
  Non Fiction/Philosopy, ISBN: 9789388118248
- Thought Vibration by William Walker Atkinson
  Non Fiction/Philosopy, ISBN: 9789389157253
- Wake Up and Live! by Dorothea Brande
  Mind, Body & Spirit, ISBN: 9789388118255
- Your Faith is Your Fortune by Neville Goddard
  Religion & Spirituality, ISBN: 9789389157260

**Search the book by its ISBN**